Blastoff! Readers are carefully developed by literacy experts to build reading stamina and move students toward fluency by combining standards-based content with developmentally appropriate text.

Level 1 provides the most support through repetition of high-frequency words, light text, predictable sentence patterns, and strong visual support.

Level 2 offers early readers a bit more challenge through varied sentences, increased text load, and text-supportive special features.

Level 3 advances early-fluent readers toward fluency through increased text load, less reliance on photos, advancing concepts, longer sentences, and more complex special features.

★ Blastoff! Universe

This edition first published in 2023 by Bellwether Media, Inc.

No part of this publication may be reproduced in whole or in part without written permission of the publisher. For information regarding permission, write to Bellwether Media, Inc., Attention: Permissions Department, 6012 Blue Circle Drive, Minnetonka, MN 55343.

Library of Congress Cataloging-in-Publication Data

Names: Sabelko, Rebecca, author.
Title: Italy / by Rebecca Sabelko.
Description: Minneapolis, MN : Bellwether Media, Inc., 2023. | Series: Blastoff! Readers : countries of the world | Includes bibliographical references and index. | Audience: Ages 5-8 | Audience: Grades 2-3 | Summary: "Relevant images match informative text in this introduction to Italy. Intended for students in kindergarten through third grade"– Provided by publisher.
Identifiers: LCCN 2022018260 (print) | LCCN 2022018261 (ebook) | ISBN 9781644877210 (library binding) | ISBN 9781648347672 (ebook)
Subjects: LCSH: Italy–Juvenile literature.
Classification: LCC DG417 .S14 2023 (print) | LCC DG417 (ebook) | DDC 945–dc23/eng/20220420
LC record available at https://lccn.loc.gov/2022018260
LC ebook record available at https://lccn.loc.gov/2022018261

Text copyright © 2023 by Bellwether Media, Inc. BLASTOFF! READERS and associated logos are trademarks and/or registered trademarks of Bellwether Media, Inc.

Editor: Elizabeth Neuenfeldt   Designer: Gabriel Hilger

Printed in the United States of America, North Mankato, MN.

Table of Contents

All About Italy	4
Land and Animals	6
Life in Italy	12
Italy Facts	20
Glossary	22
To Learn More	23
Index	24

All About Italy

Rome

Italy is a country in southern Europe. Rome is the capital.

Italy is a **peninsula**. It is shaped like a boot!

Land and Animals

The Alps mountain **range** lines northern Italy. Other mountains run across the country. **Plains** surround the long Po River.

Italy has many islands. Sicily and Sardinia are the largest.

Sicily

Po River

Size: 405 miles (652 kilometers) long
Famous For: longest river in Italy

Summers in Italy are warm. Winters are mild. Southern Italy is hot year-round.

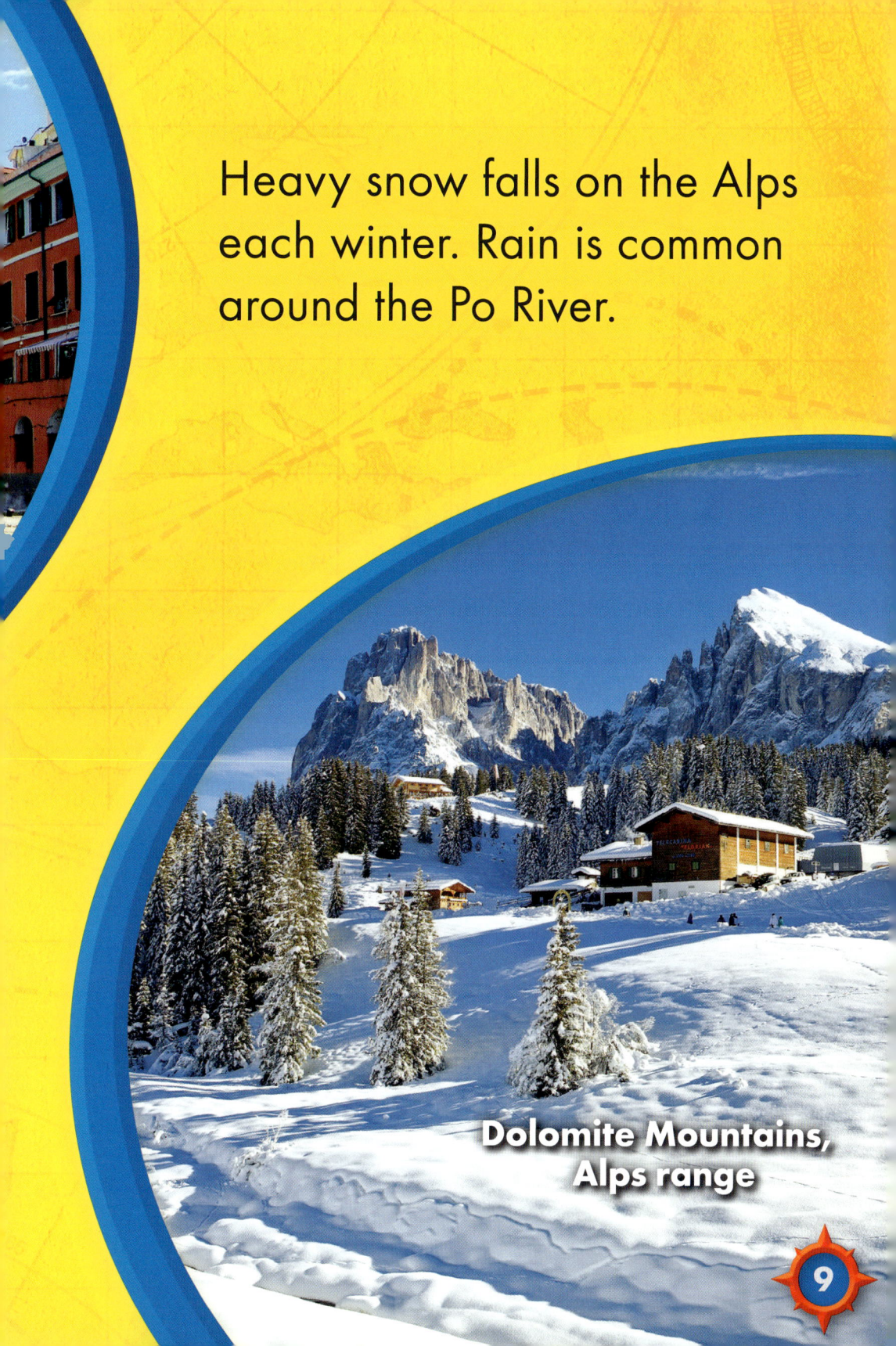

Heavy snow falls on the Alps each winter. Rain is common around the Po River.

Dolomite Mountains, Alps range

The Alps are home to ibex. Marmots dig homes in **meadows**.

alpine ibex

Animals of Italy

alpine marmot

Italian stream frog

porcelain crab

wild boar

Frogs hop through Italy's **wetlands**. Crabs crawl along the coasts. Wild boars sneak onto farms.

Life in Italy

Most people in Italy are Italian. Some people are from other countries.

Italian is the main language. But people speak **local** languages, too. Most Italians are **Christians**.

Christian church in Milan

soccer

cycling

Italians are huge soccer fans. Skiing and cycling are also popular.

Families spend Sundays together. They may visit the beach.

Italians like many foods. Spaghetti with *salsa al pomodoro* is a favorite.

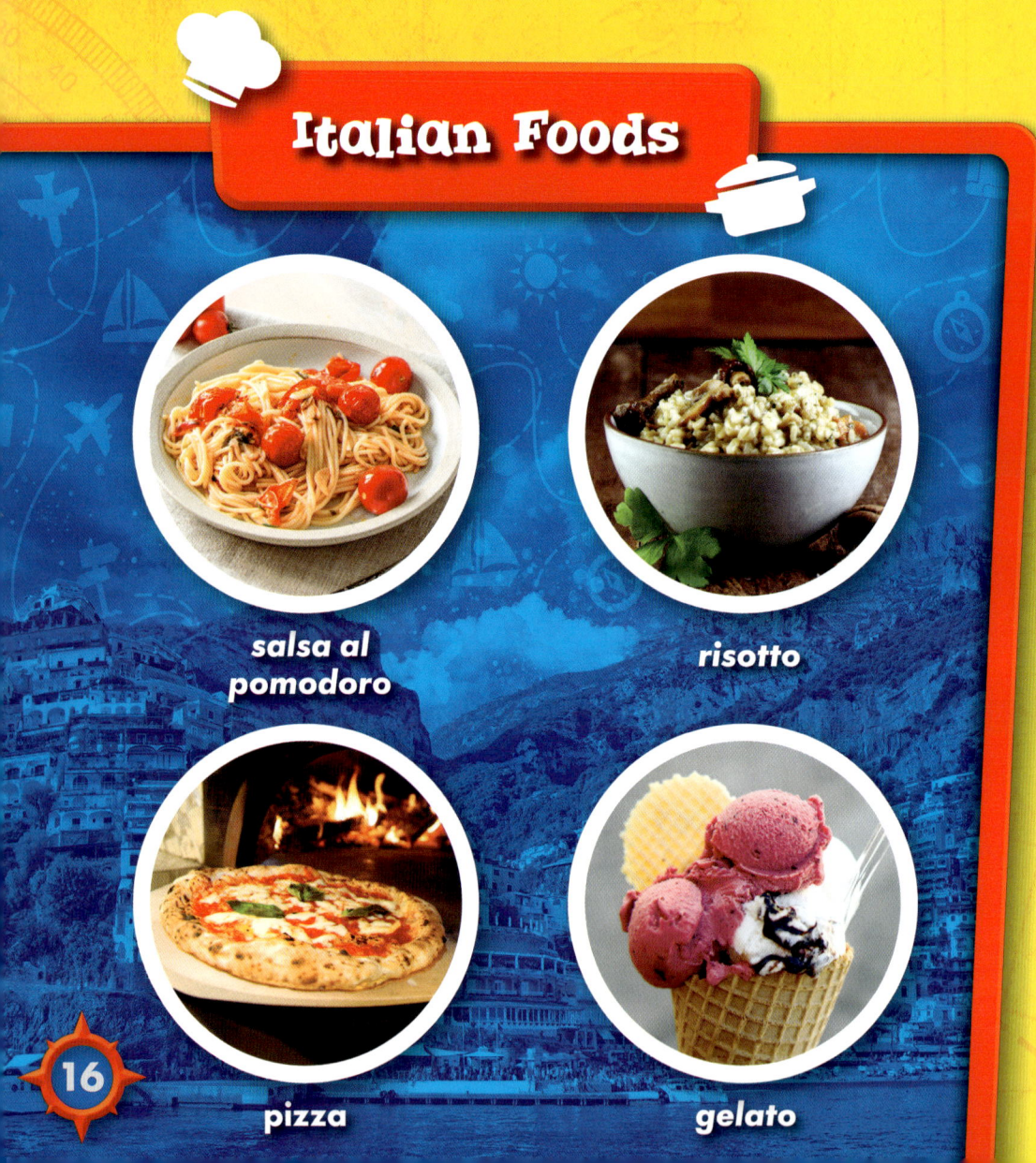

Italian Foods

salsa al pomodoro

risotto

pizza

gelato

Risotto is a tasty rice dish.
Pizza is popular across Italy.
Gelato is a frozen treat!

Carnevale is a Christian holiday. It happens in February or March before **Lent**. Big parades fill the streets.

Carnevale

Republic Day is June 2. **Festivals** across Italy honor the nation!

Italy Facts

Size:
116,348 square miles
(301,340 square kilometers)

Population:
61,095,551 (2022)

National Holiday:
Republic Day (June 2)

Main Language:
Italian

Capital City:
Rome

Famous Face

Name: Giada De Laurentiis

Famous For: an Italian chef and host on the Food Network

Religions

Muslim: 5%

other: 1%

Christian: 81%

none: 13%

Top Landmarks

Colosseum

Mount Vesuvius

Tower of Pisa

Glossary

Christians—people who believe in the words of Jesus Christ

festivals—times or events of celebration

Lent—a period of 40 days when Christians prepare for Easter

local—taking place in a certain area, city, or town

meadows—lands that are covered, or mostly covered, with grass

peninsula—a part of the land that sticks out from a larger piece of land and is almost completely surrounded by water

plains—large areas of flat land

range—a group of mountains

wetlands—areas of land that are covered with low levels of water for most of the year

To Learn More

AT THE LIBRARY

Dean, Jessica. *Italy*. Minneapolis, Minn.: Pogo, 2019.

Duling, Kaitlyn. *Alpine Ibex*. Minneapolis, Minn.: Bellwether Media, 2021.

Gleisner, Jenna Lee. *My First Look at Italian*. Minneapolis, Minn.: Bullfrog Books, 2020.

ON THE WEB

FACTSURFER

Factsurfer.com gives you a safe, fun way to find more information.

1. Go to www.factsurfer.com.
2. Enter "Italy" into the search box and click 🔍.
3. Select your book cover to see a list of related content.

Index

Alps, 6, 9, 10
animals, 10, 11
beach, 15
capital (see Rome)
Carnevale, 18, 19
Christians, 12, 18
cycling, 14
Europe, 4
families, 15
foods, 16, 17
Italy facts, 20–21
languages, 12
Lent, 18
map, 5
meadows, 10
peninsula, 5
people, 12

plains, 6
Po River, 6, 7, 9
Republic Day, 19
Rome, 4, 5
Sardinia, 6
say hello, 13
Sicily, 6
skiing, 14
soccer, 14
summers, 8
wetlands, 11
winters, 8, 9

The images in this book are reproduced through the courtesy of: Noppasin Wongchum, front cover; Javen, front cover, pp. 2-3; Diego Barbieri, p. 3; Pani Garmyder, pp. 4-5; leoks, p. 6; egadolfo, pp. 6-7; JeniFoto, pp. 8-9; Yamagiwa, p. 9; ueuaphoto, pp. 10-11; MirasWonderland, p. 11 (alpine marmot); Beatrice Prezzemoli, p. 11 (Italian stream frog); Ernie Hounshell, p. 11 (porcelain crab); mauribo, p. 11 (wild boar); Resul Muslu, p. 12; nadianb, pp. 12-13; Paolo Bona, pp. 14-15; Unomos, p. 14 (inset); TravinkovStudio, p. 15; Ostranitsa Stanislav, p. 16 (salsa al pomodoro); beats1, p. 16 (risotto); FVPhotography, p. 16 (pizza); Ra Chaeik, p. 16 (gelato); Imorthand, p. 17; federico neri, pp. 18-19; titoOnz, p. 20 (flag); s_bukley, p. 20 (Giada De Laurentiis); picturepixx, p. 21 (Colosseum); S-F, p. 21 (Mount Vesuvius); andreyspb21, p. 21 (Tower of Pisa); Tinu Weibel, pp. 22-23.